VERY SIMPLE
CHINESE

ILLUSTRATED BY
IRENE SANDERSON

VERY SIMPLE
CHINESE

By
Don Starr
&
Caroline Mason

Paul Norbury Publications
Sandgate, Folkestone, Kent, England

VERY SIMPLE CHINESE

Paul Norbury Publications
Knoll House, 35 The Crescent, Sandgate, Folkestone, Kent
England

First published 1990
© Paul Norbury Publications 1990

ISBN 0-904404-71-4

British Library Cataloguing in Publication Data
Starr, Don , 1945 -
  Very simple Chinese.
  1. Spoken Chinese language. Mandarin
  I. Title II. Mason, Caroline, 1949 -
  495.1'83421

  ISBN 0-904404-71-4

Distributed in the USA & Canada by:
The Talman Co. Inc.,
150 Fifth Avenue
New York, NY 10011

Photosetting by Visual Typesetting, Harrow, Middlesex
Printed in England by BPCC Wheaton & Co, Exeter.

Contents

Foreword

This book is a sister volume to Caroline Mason's *Simple Etiquette in China* (Paul Norbury Publications, 1989) and provides guidance on the language used in the situations encountered in that book. The reader should be assured, however, that the two books are not interdependent but are intended to stand alone or together as required.

Chapter 1 includes an introduction to the pronunciation of Chinese (Mandarin) and an outline of basic grammar. Pronunciation does present certain problems for English speakers since there are some sounds not used in English. We have tried to give a guide to these sounds based on spoken British English as well as selected American English but urge students to listen carefully to native speakers for greater accuracy. Another difficulty is tones; here again we offer a rough idea but there is no substitute for listening to the real thing. Since this is intended purely as a guide to the spoken language, it does not include Chinese characters, except in a few particularly important cases.

Chapters 3 onwards introduce the kind of language used in situations likely to be encountered by the visitor to China. Each chapter describes the language in its context and concludes with basic sentence patterns used in that context plus some additional vocabulary.

Finally, there is an Appendix dealing with numbers, times and dates and other useful specialised terms.

The language and situations are based on those of Beijing (Peking) but, for the most part, apply generally to the People's Republic of China (PRC). The basic language is the same in other Chinese-speaking areas like Taiwan, but different social, political and economic systems have resulted in some linguistic differences.

Although Chinese is the mother-tongue of more people than any other language in the world, few westerners take the trouble to learn it. You will find that even a limited knowledge is much appreciated by Chinese people, and we are sure you will find the effort worthwhile.

**DON STARR &
CAROLINE MASON**

1

The Chinese Language

There are many dialects of Chinese but what the term usually refers to is Modern Standard Chinese, often called Mandarin by westerners because it was the language used by officials in traditional China. In the People's Republic it is called *putonghua* (common language) and in Taiwan *guoyu* (national language) and in both it is the standard language used for radio, television and official functions. Mandarin was based on the dialect of Beijing and spread by migration to north-east, central and west China but was not used in the coastal areas from which most overseas Chinese came. So if you try out your Chinese at your local restaurant and get no response do not be disappointed — the owners probably come from Hong Kong and speak Cantonese or Hakka.

To westerners Chinese has two particularly unusual features: its writing system and its tones.

THE WRITING SYSTEM

Instead of an alphabet of twenty or thirty letters Chinese is written with many thousands of different characters each of which originally represented a whole word. Unlike the letters of an alphabet, characters represent meaning, not sound, so they can be used in different dialects or even completely different languages to convey the same meaning. This enabled the Japanese, Koreans and Vietnamese to borrow Chinese characters and write down their own very different languages. This is rather like our use of numbers: 1,2,3 etc. mean the same to a Norwegian, a Russian and an Italian when they see them written down, but they all pronounce them differently.

Traditional writing was in vertical lines from top to bottom and right to left, so with a book printed in that style you start from what to us would be the back. It is now usual to write in horizontal lines and from left to right, as in the West.

In the years after 1949 the government of the People's Republic of China introduced simplified versions of many characters to make them easier to learn and write, but other areas, like Taiwan and Hong Kong, still use the original 'full' characters.

TONES

The number of different sounds in Chinese is much fewer than in English and many words have the same pronunciation. Chinese people play games making up little stories composed of words all pronounced the same. For example 'A poet by the name of Shi, who lived in a stone house, liked lions and swore that he would eat ten lions' can be expressed in words all pronounced *shi*.

One way of distinguishing words which otherwise sound the same is by the use of tones. In Modern Standard Chinese there are four tones:

1st is *high level*, indicated by ¯ above the vowel in romanisation, e.g. *mā* 'mother', on a pitch similar to a 'la' when one sings 'tra la la'.

2nd is *rising*, indicated by ´, e.g. *má* 'hemp', and is pitched like the rising 'o' in 'Coming?'.

3rd is *falling and rising*, indicated by ˇ e.g. *mǎ* 'horse' and is the lowest in initial pitch and the longest in duration. It is like the word 'well' which is drawn out as in 'Well, I don't know'.

4th is *falling*, indicated by ` e.g. *mà* 'to curse', and is pitched like a short, sharp 'No'.

Unstressed syllables often lose their tone and become neutral. Tones sometimes change to show a difference in meaning or function; *bù* 'not' and *yī* 'one' are exceptional in that they change tone according to the following tone.

PRONUNCIATION

A romanised version of Chinese is used throughout this book as an alphabetic guide to pronunciation. The romanisation used here is *pinyin*, the standard PRC system, but elsewhere you may meet Wade-Giles, the older system. For example, the name of the late Chairman of the Chinese Communist Party is Mao Zedong in *pinyin* and Mao Tse-tung in Wade-Giles. However, Chinese themselves write in characters and few are familiar with romanisation, reading it only with difficulty.

PINYIN GUIDE

The following is based on British English but is only a rough guide; the learner should listen to a native speaker to acquire greater accuracy. For American English speakers alternatives are indicated where appropriate (A.E.).

The consonants b,d,f,g (always hard as in 'go'), h,j,k,l,m,n,p,s,t,w,ch and sh are similar to their pronunciations in English. The exceptions are:

c is like ts in let's

q is like ch in cheese

r is a cross between the English r as in crew and si in vision

x is like sh in sheep but with the lips drawn more tightly back and with more air through the teeth

z is like ds in bids

zh is like j in June

Vowels, compound vowels and other finals are as follows:

a is between a in map and a in car (A.E.: like a in father)

e is like er in her except when followed by ng when it is like the er in sister (A.E.: like a in about but longer)

i following most letters is like ee in see but following z,c,s,zh,ch,sh and r it is very like ir in bird but shorter and sharper (in A.E. following z,c etc. it is like ir in sir)

o is like a in what (in A.E. like wa in wall) except when followed by ng when it is like the oo in look

u is like oo in spoon except when it follows, j,q,x and y or when it is written ü, in which case it is like ew in lewd (the latter also applies to uan and un).

ai is like eye

ei is like ay in day

ie (and ye) is like ye in yet

iu is like yo as in yodel

ia is like ya in yard (A.E. like ya in yacht)

ian (and *yan*) is like yen

in is like *ean* in bean but shorter and sharper

iang (and *yang*) is like Yan in Yankee (A.E. *ee* as in see + *ang*)

iong (and *yong*) is like the *ee* of see, but shorter, + *ong*

ou is like *ow* in low

ua (and *wa*) is *oo* as in look + a as above (in A.E. is like *wa* in wander)

uo (and *wo*) is like *wa* in want (in A.E. is like *Wa* in Walter)

uai (and *wai*) is like *wi* in wine

ui (and *wei*) is like way

uan (and *wan*) is like the *oo* of too, but shorter, + *an*

uang (and *wang*) is like a short *oo* as in look + *ong* of wrong

un is like the *oo* in look + en in oven (A.E. like *wen* in Owen)

ue and *üe* (also *yue*) are pronounced like you + e of fetch

Chinese was originally more or less mono-syllabic: one syllable = one character = one whole word. In modern Chinese, one syllable still = one character, but many words are composed of two or more syllables and hence two or more characters. Most syllables are composed of an initial consonant (including *zh, ch, sh*) followed by a vowel element, although it is possible to have a syllable which consists of only the vowel element. There may be a final consonant after the vowel, but only *n* and *ng* can occur in this position, except in Beijing where it is common to add an r to many words, for example, *lǚguǎn* becomes *lǚguǎnr*. An apostrophe is used to show the syllable break where alternative readings are possible: *ping'an* shows it is *ping* + *an* not *pin* + *gan* for example.

BASIC GRAMMAR

The following attempts to give an idea of some of the basic patterns of Chinese. You may prefer to go straight on to the situations and come back to this for reference.

The basic structure of Chinese is not as different from English as you might imagine and there are none of the complicated conjugations and declensions that make many European languages so difficult to learn. However, the fact that Chinese and English do not have any common roots does mean that almost every item of vocabulary is different and has to be learnt individually.

Word order is similar to English with subject-verb-object as the basic pattern:
  Wǒ hē chá I drink tea

Adjectives come before the nouns they describe and adverbs mostly come before the verb:
  *Wǒ <u>píngcháng</u> hē **lǜ** chá*
  I <u>usually</u> drink **green** tea

In Chinese, unlike English, the time (when) and place element come before the verb and in that order:
  *Wǒ **shí diǎn zhōng** <u>zài shíchǎng</u> jiàn tā.*
  I'm meeting him <u>in the market</u> at **10 o'clock.**

The time phrase may come before or after the subject, place always comes after. Time duration, however, is treated differently to time when, and follows the verb, like an object:
  Wǒ děng le sān ge zhōngtou.
  I waited for three hours.
Unlike English, questions with question words (who, what, etc) have the same order as a statement. *Tā shì <u>shéi</u>?* <u>Who</u> is he?

English verbs conjugate in a tense system but Chinese verbs do not, so *hē* can mean 'drink/s', 'drank', 'am/is/are drinking', 'have/has drunk', 'will drink', etc. Context is often enough to make clear which aspect is intended but there are other ways (see *le* below). There is no plural form for nouns so in the following sentence *bǐ* 'pen' can mean one pen or more than one, whereas in English we have to tie ourselves down to either singular or plural:

Wǒ mǎi bǐ I am buying a pen/some pens

Of course Chinese can be precise, if necessary — by specifying a particular number of pens, for example.

Particles

Chinese gets over some of the problems caused by the absence of inflection by using particles and other words which have no substantive meaning and cannot be directly translated but have important grammatical functions. Here are some of the major ones (note carefully the position in the sentence).

ma when added to the end of a statement turns it into a question:
   Nǐ píngcháng hē lǜ chá ma?
   Do you usually drink green tea?

ba forms a suggestion or a supposition:
   Nǐ hē chá ba   Have some tea
   Tāmen yě qù Běijīng ba
   They must be going to Beijing too
ne forms a tag question or else indicates an action is in progress:
   Wǒ hē chá, nǐ ne?
   I'm having some tea, how about you?
   Wǒ hē chá ne
   I'm just having some tea
a is commonly used at the end of a wide variety of sentences expressing approval, realisation, doubt or surprise, and may be

in sentences with question words (where *ma* cannot be used):

Zhè zhǒng lù chá zhēn hǎohē a
This kind of green tea is really delicious
Tā shì shéi a
Who is he?

de used before a noun at its simplest indicates possession, like 's in English

péngyou de bǐ   friend's pen

but is also used to indicate possession of particular attributes and frequently comes between adjectives or adjectival phrases and the nouns they describe:

hěn hǎohē de chá   very delicious tea
Nǐ zuótiān zài Běijīng mǎi de chá . . .
The tea which you bought in Beijing yesterday . . .

de is also used to make adjectives and verbs into nouns, in English ' . . . one' :

lù de   a green one
Tā mǎi de shì lù de
The one he bought is a green one

le can come immediately after a verb or at the end of a sentence or phrase.

In the former case it indicates realisation or accomplishment:

Tā mǎi le yì bāo lù chá
He bought/has bought a packet of green tea

In the latter case *le* implies that what is said has relevance for the current situation. This is a difficult concept for English speakers.
Tā mǎi chá le   He's bought the tea
(i.e. so we can go now)

This type of *le* is also common with adjectival (stative) verbs (see below) and suggests a change of state:

Shù dōu lù le
The trees have all turned green

bǎ may be used where there is a sense of disposal to change the subject-verb-object order to subject –*bǎ* + object – verb :

Wǒ bǎ chá bāoqilai le
I have wrapped up the tea

This *bǎ* is a different character to the suggestive one above, and apart from position is distinguished in speech by having a full tone. The suggestive *ba*, like most other particles above, is neutral in tone.

Negation

Negation is produced by putting *bù* before the verb:
    Wǒ bù hē chá I don't drink tea

The only exception is the verb *yǒu* 'to have', which takes *méi* :
    Wǒ méi yǒu chá I don't have any tea

For realised action, where the affirmative verb would take a *le* (see *le* above), the negative takes *méi* or *méi yǒu*
 Nǐ hē chá le ma Have you had some tea?
 Wǒ méi (yǒu) hē chá I haven't had any tea
or just   *Méi yǒu* No
Note that the *le* is omitted where there is *méi*, but can be used with *bù*:
    Wǒ méi hē chá I haven't had any tea
                (unrealised)
 Wǒ bù hē chá le I don't drink tea any more
      or I shan't have any tea
    (No thanks, I've had enough now.)

Because there are no tenses in Chinese what is a verb is far less clear cut and adverbs, adjectives (stative verbs) and prepositions may also in some cases be negated by *bù*
         bù cháng   not often
          bù hǎo   not good
   bú zuò (fēijī)   not by (plane)

17

Asking Questions

There are four main question forms:

1. the *ma* question where *ma* is added to the end of a statement:

> *Nǐ hē chá ma*   Do you drink tea?

2. the choice-type question:

> *Nǐ hē bù hē chá?*   Do you drink tea?

Nǐ hē chá le méiyou   Have you had any tea?
> (= *Nǐ hē méi hē chá?*)

This form can only be used where the question lies in the verb:

> *Nǐ cháng hē chá ma?*   Do you often drink tea?

can only be expressed with *ma* because the question is whether you *often* drink tea, not whether you drink it or not

3. The question word:

> *Nǐ yào hē shénme?*
> What would you like to drink?

such questions can take the final particle *a* but not *ma*

4. The either . . . or . . . question using *háishi*

> *Nǐ hē chá háishi (hē) kāfēi?*
> Would you like tea or coffee?

if there is no verb *shì* ('is') is used in the first part

> *Shì chá háishi kāfēi?*   Is it tea or coffee?

Adjectives or Stative Verbs?

Chinese adjectives come before the noun like English ones:

> *lǜ chá*   green tea

and a few are restricted to this role but most can be used as stative verbs, i.e. *kuài* means both 'fast' and 'is fast'

> *kuài chē*   fast bus/train (express)
> *chē kuài*   the bus is fast

in the latter case, unless a comparative sense is intended, it is usual to add *hěn* 'very' in the affirmative;

18

chē hěn kuài　the bus is (very) fast
but the negative is simply
　　　chē bú kuài　the bus is not fast

To be and not to be

As we have just seen, the Chinese equivalent of the verb 'is', *shì*, is more limited in usage than in English. It says that two things are equivalent:

　　　Zhè shì lǜ chá　This is green tea

Shì is not used to denote existence, For this Chinese uses *yǒu* 'have' (like the French 'il y a').

　Zhèr yǒu lǜ chá　There is some green tea here (*zhè* = this thing and *zhèr* = here)

There are no Chinese equivalents to the English words 'yes' and 'no', but *shì* and *bú shì* are the nearest to them.

Shì bú shì, the choice-type question formed with *shì*, is very useful as a tag question seeking verification

　　　Wǒmen zuò fēijī qù, shì bú shì?
　　　We are going by plane, aren't we?

In questions or statements concerning: the time of an action, the location or purpose, the instrument used, the person carrying out the action and similar points (often involving the use of a preposition) *shì . . . de* (often abbreviated to just *. . . de*) is added to the basic sentence. It usually refers to past events:

　Tā shì jǐ diǎn dào de?　What time did he arrive?
　Bā diǎn bàn dào de　At half past eight.

Measure Words

As we have seen Chinese nouns are generic and hence less specific than their English equivalents, so when they are being referred to specifically they take measure words or counters. The situation is similar to that of the

19

word 'cattle' in English where we do not say 'ten cattle' but insert the measure word 'head of', as in 'ten head of cattle.' Almost all nouns have specific measures but the commonest is *ge*: if in doubt use that.

Measures must be used between numbers and nouns, and between *zhè** 'this,' *nà** 'that,' *nǎ** 'which?' *jǐ* 'how many?' *měi* 'each ' and the following noun.

Sān ge péngyou lái le   Three friends came
Nèi liàng lǜ chē shì wǒ de
That green car is mine
Nǐ mǎi jǐ zhī bǐ?
How many pens are you buying?

A list of common measures is given in the Appendix.

*Zhè is often pronounced *zhèi* before a measure and, similarly, *nà* and *nǎ* may be pronounced *nèi* and *něi*. You should be familiar with both types of pronunciation, so we include both in this book. There is no difference in meaning.

Useful Phrases

Nǐ hǎo	Hello
Huānyíng	Welcome
Xièxie	Thank you
Bú kèqi	You're welcome
Duìbuqǐ	I'm sorry, Excuse me
Méi guānxi	Think nothing of it, it doesn't matter
Qǐng wèn . . .	May I ask you . . .
Qǐng nǐ . . .	Will you please . . .
Zàijiàn	Goodbye

Question words

shéi	who
shénme	what
shénme shíhou	when
zěnme	how, how come

zěnme yàng	in what way, how
wèishénme	why
(yīnwèi)	(because)
năr	where
duōshao	how many, how much
jĭ (+measure)	how many (used for numerals up to 10)

Prepositions

These are sometimes called coverbs and in a negative sentence it is normally the preposition that is negated (with *bù*), not the main verb.

zài	at, in, on
cóng	from
dào	to
zuò	by (bus, train etc.)
yòng	with (instrument)
gēn	with, accompanying (a person)

2

Arriving in China

The majority of western travellers arrive in China through one of its international airports. If you are travelling on business, you will probably be met by your Chinese contacts. If you are going with a tour group, then the group leader will deal with arrival formalities for you. Independent travellers have no such help, of course, but will find that on the whole they can negotiate passport control and customs without knowing any Chinese. However, the following may be useful:

> *Qǐng wèn, yínháng zài nǎr?*
> Excuse me, where is the bank?

or *Qǐng wèn, chūzūchē zài nǎr?*
> Excuse me, where are the taxis?

If you need to find a telephone, you say

> *Qǐng wèn, gōngyòng diànhuà zài nǎr?*
> Excuse me, where is the public phone?

When you change your money at the bank (Chinese currency cannot legally be taken into China) you will be given Foreign Exchange Certificates, or FECs (*wàihuì* in Chinese). These are different from the normal official currency of China *Rénmínbì* (RMB), and you will find that Chinese people are eager to obtain FECs because they can be used to purchase imported goods not available for *Rénmínbì*. Carry a range of FEC denominations and refuse to accept RMB change except in small amounts. It is in practice less valuable and is not convertible when you leave the country.

There is a list of foreign currencies in the Appendix.

Signs you will see:

rùkǒu 入口
entrance

chūkǒu 出口
exit

cèsuǒ 厕所
lavatory

gōngyòng 公用电话
diànhuà
public phone

nán 男
male

nǚ 女
female

Many signs are accompanied by pictures — the silhouette of a woman's head as the sign for 'Ladies,' for instance — which is very helpful.

If you have to catch a connecting flight, remember that C.A.A.C., China's airline, does not always run to the precise schedules advertised, so be prepared to wait. And bear in mind that it is very difficult to make onward bookings within China. The first task when you arrive at a destination in China is to arrange your departure! (See Ch.5 Getting Around.)

To check when your flight leaves, you can ask:

> *Qù (Shànghǎi) de fēijī jǐ diǎn qǐfēi?*
> What time does the plane to (Shanghai) take off?
> (For times, please see the Appendix)

In reply, you may hear the words *děng yí děng*, which means 'wait a moment'.

It is the custom in China to go to the point of departure to see one's guests off — if anyone takes you to the airport you might hear them say:

> *yí lù shùn fēng* or *yí lù píng' ān*,
> both of which mean 'Bon Voyage.'

If you decide to take a taxi from the airport, and you know the name of your destination, say:

> *Wǒ yào qù (Běijīng Fàndiàn)*
> I'd like to go to (the Beijing Hotel)

If you are less sure of yourself, get someone to write down your destination in characters, show it to the driver and say:

> *Wǒ yào qù zhèi ge dìfang*
> I want to go to this place

All authorised taxis are metered, so check that the driver turns his meter on as you set off. When you arrive at your destination you should of course be able to read the fare on the meter, but if you want to check you can say:

> *Duōshao qián?*   How much?

The taxi driver will want payment in FEC, and will give you a receipt. In theory, there is no tipping, but in practice it is becoming increasingly common.

If you want the taxi to wait for you, say to the driver:

> *Qǐng děng yí děng*   Please wait

(There is more on Money in the section on Shopping in Ch.6)

Basic sentences and vocabulary

Where have you come from?
> *Nǐ cóng nǎr lái*

I've come from (Hong Kong)
> *Wǒ cóng (Xiānggǎng) lái*

Why have you come to China?
> *Nǐ lái Zhōngguó zuò shénme?*

I've come on business/vacation
> *Wǒ lái bànshì / dùjià*

Please sign here   *Qǐng nǐ zài zhèr qiānmíng*

Is all your luggage here?
> *Nǐ de xíngli dōu zài zhèr ma?*

It's all here   *Dōu zài zhèr*

Excuse me, where is (the bank)?
> *Qǐngwèn, (yínháng) zài nǎr?*

Over there   *Zài nèr*

I want to go to (the Peace Hotel)
> *Wǒ yào qù (Hépíng Fàndiàn)*

How much is it?   *Duōshao qián?*

passport	*hùzhào*
passport number	*hùzhào hàomǎ*
visa	*qiānzhèng*
customs	*hǎiguān*
customs duty	*guānshuì*
duty free	*miǎnshuì*
nationality	*guójí*
immigration card	*rùjìng dēngjì kǎ*

3

At your hotel

There are several grades of hotel in China. The top hotels are called *fàndiàn*, the next grade *bīnguǎn* and then *lǚguǎn*. Basic hostel-type accommodation is also available. In the big hotels it should be easy to find English-speaking staff (learning English is very much in vogue in China at present), but in hostels it may be difficult. Tour-groups will of course be looked after by their leaders, but if you are on your own you might want to ask:

> *Yǒu fángjiān ma?*
> Do you have a room available?

And, if there is, to follow it up with:

> *Duōshao qián?*
> How much is it?

The price will probably be quoted in *yuán* — the formal name for the unit of Chinese currency. (See the section on Numerals in the Appendix.)

When you want to check out, you can ask for the bill by saying:

Qǐng gěi wǒ jié zhàng
Please make up the bill for me

In the lift, the attendant may ask you *Jǐ lóu?*, meaning 'Which floor?' You can answer with *èr (sān, sì) lóu* (first, (second, third) floor) etc. Remember that English ground-floor is Chinese first floor.

Signs you will see:

饭店   邮局   电话   电梯
Fàndiàn   *Yóujú*   *Diànhuà*   *Diàntī*
Hotel   Post Office   Telephone   Lift

服务台   餐厅
fúwùtái   *cāntīng*
service desk   dining-room

Most large hotels in China contain a number of shops, selling a wide range of goods from European-type breads to cosmetics, films and gifts. There are also usually a hair-dresser's and a post-office, and it is possible to make international phone-calls and send telexes.

If you want to find the post-office, say:
    Yóujú zài nǎr?   Where is the post-office?

For international mail it is a good idea to ask someone to write the name of the country in Chinese characters on the envelope. Chinese envelopes and some stamps are not pre-glued — you will need to stick them down with glue from the pot provided.

To buy stamps, say:
    Wǒ yào mǎi yóupiào
    I'd like to buy some stamps

To specify how many, use a numeral plus measure-word:
    sì zhāng yóupiào   four stamps

To specify what denomination, add the price plus *de*:

> *sì zhāng yí kuài liù de yóupiào*
> four ¥1.60 stamps

If you want to know the price of a letter to a particular destination, say:

> *Jìdào (Měiguó) yí fēng (hángkōng) xìn, duōshao qián?*
> How much is it to send an (airmail) letter to (America)?

Parcels should be left open for inspection before being tied up securely. It is a good idea to send them by registered post.

Phone-calls can be made from main post-offices, but it is easier to make them from your hotel — especially as you may have to wait a long time for an international call to be connected if there is no IDD. Explain that you want to make a call by saying:

> *Wǒ yào dǎ ge (chángtú) diànhuà*
> I'd like to make a (long-distance) call

You may be told:

> *méi yǒu rén jiē* — there's no answer
> or *dǎ bú tōng* — I can't get through
> or *zhàn xiàn* — the line is engaged

If you are calling within China, the usual expression for 'Hello' is *wèi*, often repeated a couple of times. This is also what the person answering the call will say.

To ask for Li Yang, say:

> *Lǐ Yáng zài ma?*   Is Li Yang there?

But since telephoning in China is very much a hit-and-miss affair, probably the most useful phrase you will need is:

> *Nǐ néng bāng wǒ dǎ ge diànhuà ma?*
> Can you help me make a phone call?

Basic Sentences and Vocabulary

Do you have any rooms?   *Yǒu fángjiān ma?*
Do you want a single or a double?
Nǐ yào dānrén fángjiān háishi shuāngrén fángjiān?
I want a (single room)
                Wǒ yào yí ge (dānrén fángjiān)
Your room is no (517) on the (5th) floor
    Nǐ de fángjiān shì (wǔ) lóu (wǔ yāo qī) hào
How much per day is it?
                        Yì tiān duōshao qián?
¥ 180 per day
                    Yì tiān yìbǎi bāshí kuài qián.
Does it have a bathroom?   *Yǒu xǐzǎojiān ma?*
How long are you intending to stay?
                    Nǐ dǎsuàn zhù duō jiǔ?
Two or three days   *Liǎng sān tiān*
Please fill in a registration form
                    Qǐng nǐ tián dēngjì biǎo
Where is (the dining-room)   *(Cāntīng) zài nǎr?*
Can I (change money)?   *Néng (huàn qián) ma?*
Can you help me . . .   *Nǐ néng bāng wǒ . . .*
Do you take credit cards?
                    Néng yòng xìnyòng kǎ ma?
There are no (towels)   *Méi yǒu (máojīn)*
book (in advance) a room   *yùdìng fángjiān*
single room   *dānrén fángjiān*
double room   *shuāngrén fángjiān*
bathroom   *xǐzǎojiān*
register   *dēngjì*
registration form   *dēngjì biǎo*
passport   *hùzhào*
. . . floor   *. . . lóu / céng*
dining room   *cāntīng*
service desk   *fúwùtái*
bar   *jiǔbā*
lift   *diàntī*
post office   *yóujú*
letter   *xìn* (measure *fēng*)
airmail (letter)   *hángkōng (xìn)*
ordinary letter   *píngxìn*

seamail *hǎilù*
parcel (postal) *yóubāo*
register (letter) *guàhào* (*xìn*)
post-card *míngxìnpiàn*
post to (France) *jìdào* (*Fǎguó*)
telegram *diànbào*
telex *diànchuán*
fax *chuánzhēn*
key *yàoshi*
heating *nuǎnqì*
air conditioning *lěngqì*
blanket *tǎnzi*
towel *máojīn*
laundry (clothes to be washed) *yào xǐ de yīfu*
. . . is broken, doesn't work . . . *huài le*
luggage *xínglǐ*
map *dìtú*
film *jiāojuǎn*
battery *diànchí*

4

Talking about yourself

Chinese people tend to be very curious about foreigners, especially in places where they are seen only rarely, but it is a friendly curiosity and — because so many of them are learning English now — they may be keen to engage you in conversation.

After the introductory *Nǐ hǎo* 'Hello', you might be asked if you can speak Chinese: *Nǐ huì shuō Hànyǔ ma?* To which you might want to reply *Bú huì* 'I can't, or perhaps *Yìdiǎn(r)* 'A little.'

If you are asked where you come from *Nǐ shì nǎguó rén?* 'Which country do you come from?', you can say *Wǒ shì Yīngguó rén* 'I am English' (literally 'I am England person'). (For other countries, see the Appendix.)

To tell someone your name, say either *Wǒ xìng (Smith)* 'My surname is (Smith)', or *Wǒ jiào (John Smith),* 'My name is (John Smith).'

Remember that Chinese names always start with the surname followed by the given name. Thus, Wang Mingde is Mr Wang, not Mr Mingde. Similarly, titles such as Miss (*Xiǎojie*), Teacher (*Lǎoshī*) or Manager (*Jīnglǐ*) also all follow the surname. It is more polite in formal situations to address people by their surname and title, e.g. *Wáng Júzhǎng* (Bureau Director Wang), than by their full name. *Lǎo* 'old' and *Xiǎo* 'young' precede the surname, e.g. *Lǎo Wáng* 'Old Wang', *Xiǎo Lǐ* 'Young Li', and are used informally to address older (but not necessarily old!) and younger colleagues. Only relatives and close friends call each other by their given names.

You will find that Chinese people are not at all inhibited when it comes to discussing such subjects as age, salaries and marital status. Be prepared for questions like *Nǐ duō dà niánjì le?* 'How old are you?', to which you answer by giving the appropriate number plus *suì*, year of age. *Wǒ sānshí èr suì*, for example, means 'I'm thirty-two.' (See Appendix for numerals.) The cult of youth has not yet hit China — if asked to guess someone's age, do not knock ten years off to be polite, or they may take it as a suggestion that you think they are inexperienced and immature.

You might find it easier to talk about your family if you have taken along photos of them. Some useful expressions in this context include *Jiéhūn le ma?* 'Are you married?'; *Jiéhūn le* 'Yes', or *Méi yǒu* 'No'; *Nǐ yǒu jǐ ge háizi?* 'How many children have you got?'; *Wǒ yǒu sān ge háizi* 'I have got three children.'

On the topic of work, you could ask someone *Nǐ zuò shénme gōngzuò?* 'What job do you do?'. The answer might be, for example, *Wǒ shì kuàijì* 'I'm an accountant'.

Chinese people often think of themselves in terms of their *dānwèi*, or work-unit, so that is another term you need to be familiar with. It can refer to a school, factory, or whatever organisation they work for.

If you are in China on business take some name-cards, *míngpiàn*, with you. Their use is very widespread in China and covers groups like teachers and civic officials, who would not normally use name-cards in the West. If you and your company expect to have regular contacts with Chinese, have a Chinese version printed: but do take advice on the characters used to transliterate the names, otherwise you could end up as 'Mr Big Nose of the Always Breaks Down Machine Tool Co.' or something similarly inappropriate. On first meeting say *Nǐ hǎo, wǒ shì Yīngguó (Arlington) Gōngsī de (John Smith). Zhè shì wǒ de míngpiàn*, 'Hello. I am (John Smith) from the British (Arlington) Company. This is my card'.

Basic sentences and vocabulary

Are you (American)?
Nǐ shì (Měiguó) rén ma?
No, I'm (Australian)
Búshì, wǒ shì (Àozhōu) rén
Can you speak (English)?
Nǐ huì shuō (Yīngyǔ) ma?
What is your name?
Nǐ jiào shénme míngzi?
My name is (John Smith)
Wǒ jiào (John Smith)
How old are you? *Nǐ duō dà niánjì le?*
I'm (thirty-seven) *Wǒ (sānshí qī suì)*
What work do you do?
Nǐ zuò shénme gōngzuò?
I am a (lawyer) *Wǒ shì (lǜshī)*
Where is your home? *Nǐ de jiā zài nǎr?*

I live in (Melbourne)   *Wǒ zhù zài (Mò'ěrběn)*
I have (a younger brother and a younger sister)
           Wǒ yǒu (yí ge dìdi, yí ge mèimei)

Relatives

mother	*māma*
father	*bàba*
spouse	*àirén*
wife	*tàitai* or
	fūrén
husband	*zhàngfu*
son	*érzi*
grandson	*sūnzi*
daughter	*nǚ'ér*
granddaughter	*sūnnǚ'ér*
older brother	*gēge*
younger brother	*dìdi*
older sister	*jiějie*
younger sister	*mèimei*
boyfriend	*nán péngyou*
girlfriend	*nǚ péngyou*
family, home	*jiā*

Occupations

accountant	*kuàjì*
businessman/	
woman	*shāngrén*
doctor	*dàifu* or *yīshēng*
engineer	*gōngchéngshī*
lawyer	*lǜshī*
student	*xuésheng*
teacher	*lǎoshī*

5

Getting Around

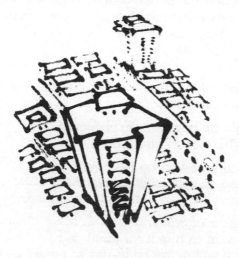

Local maps are available in hotels but are not necessarily very informative. Traditional Chinese cities were built on a grid pattern and so Chinese have a much better sense of compass direction than many westerners and will often give directions by points of the compass:

> *Láojià, nǐ néng gàosu wǒ Hépíng Fàndiàn zài nǎr ma?*
> Excuse me, can you tell me where the Peace Hotel is?

> *Yìzhi wàng běi zǒu, dào le hónglǜdēng nèr wàng dōng guǎi.*
> Walk straight north, when you get to the traffic lights turn east.

There is a certain loss of face involved in not knowing, so you may be sent off in the wrong direction by someone reluctant to admit they are not sure. Do not believe everything you are told!

The most interesting way round cities is on foot. In spite of rising crime levels, Chinese cities are still fairly safe day or night. There is, so far, little violent crime but there is not the total honesty of fifteen years ago (when visitors had returned to them things they were trying to throw away), so beware of pickpockets in crowded places.

If you want to travel like the locals you can hire a bicycle. Ask:

> *Wǒ zài nǎr néng zū zìxíngchē*
> Where can I hire a bike?

You will be asked by the hirer:
> *Yào zū duō cháng shíjiān?*
> How long do you want to hire it for?

> *Yào zū (yí) tiān*
> I want to hire it for (one) day

and you will be asked to pay a deposit *yājīn*.

> *Yājīn èrshí kuài qián*
> The deposit is ¥20

Park your bicycle in a bicycle park (a roped-off area on the road or pavement) where the attendant will charge you a few *fēn*, and *always* lock it securely.

It is possible to hire cars but usually better to take a taxi even for long distances. Traffic conditions can be chaotic and many cyclists have little road sense and turn into the path of cars without warning. If there is an accident, and there are many, the car driver is usually assumed to be at fault and faces severe punishment and heavy compensation claims. Even if you want to travel out of town it is likely to be better to take a taxi. Tell the driver where and when you want to go and negotiate a price with him.

Wǒmen (sān ge rén) yào qù (Chángchéng hé Shísānlíng), shàngwǔ (bā diǎn) chūfā xiàwǔ (liù diǎn) huídào fàndiàn lái, duōshao qián?

We (three) want to go to (the Great Wall and the Ming tombs), starting out at (8.00) am and returning to the hotel at (6.00) pm. How much will it be? (See Appendix for times)

Many drivers will be pleased at the prospect of a day out paid in *wàihuì*, but you may need to haggle.

Èrbǎi kuài tài guì le, wǒ zuì duō néng gěi yíbǎi wǔshí kuài

¥200 is too expensive, the most I can pay is ¥150.

Taxis are metered for local trips, so check that the driver has started the meter and, if not, say:

Qǐng nǐ dǎkāi jìjiàqì
Please start the meter

Signs you will see:

火车站
huǒchē zhàn
station (train)

(飞)机场
(fēi)jī chǎng
airport

售票处
shòupiào chù
booking office

软卧
ruǎnwò
soft sleeper

硬卧
yìngwò
hard sleeper

出租车
chūzūchē
taxi

It is usually a fixed price for the first 4 kilometres and per kilometre thereafter. The per kilometre price varies with the size of the taxi and should be shown in the rear passenger door window. Taxis have a taxi sign on the roof with the characters for *chūzūchē*, taxi, and usually the word in English too. However, because drivers prefer foreigners with FECs to Chinese with RMB they are reluctant to stop in the street, but congregate at the big hotels. If you want a taxi it is best to go to a big hotel, friendship store or other building frequented by foreigners.

City buses are very crowded, dirty and slow but also very cheap. Bus stops have the names of all the stops on the route, *lù*, with the relevant one indicated.

To make sure ask:

> *Dào (Běijīng Fàndiàn) néng zuò jǐ lù chē?*
> What bus(es) can I take to the (Beijing Hotel)?

> *Sān lù, qī lù, shíwǔ lù dōu kěyǐ.*
> No. 3, no. 7 and no. 15 are all O.K.

When you pay the conductress ask to be told when to get off:

> *Dào le (Běijīng Fàndiàn) néng gàosu wǒ ma?*
> Can you tell me when we reach the (Beijing Hotel)?

To make your way through the crush of passengers to the exit door shout:

> *xiàchē, xiàchē*
> I'm getting off

There are also private minibuses which are quicker than public buses and guarantee a seat but are many times more expensive, although still very reasonable by western standards. Many are painted white or cream with a green stripe and are nicknamed *miànbāochē* 'bread buses' because of the supposed resemblance. You are more likely to be overcharged on these, so watch what others pay.

There are long-distance buses to remote areas but for most visitors train *huǒchē* or plane *fēijī* is the norm for longer journeys. Tickets for both can be in short supply.

Train tickets are for a specific train, so do not miss the train you have booked. There are three classes: soft sleeper *ruǎnwò*, hard sleeper *yìngwò* and hard seat *yìngzuò*. Soft sleeper offers separate compartments with 4 berths, hard sleeper has six berths in open compartments. Since trains are slow and distances long, hard seat is not recommended, except for brief journeys. Trains have good dining cars *–cānchē*. In general you cannot buy return tickets, *láihuí piào*, only singles, *dānchéng piào*.

When you arrive in a town for a short visit, buying an onward ticket should be a first priority. Ask at the station *huǒchē zhàn* when you arrive:

Yǒu míngtiān qù (Chéngdū) de huǒchē piào ma?
Are there any train tickets to (Chengdu) tomorrow?
Shénme yàngr de piào?
What kind of ticket?
Ruǎnwò Soft sleeper
Méi yǒu ruǎnwò, yìngwò kěyǐ ma?
There are no soft sleepers, will hard sleeper do?
Hǎo O.K.
Jǐ zhāng? How many?
(Liǎng) zhāng (Two)

The Chinese national air line *Mínháng* (presently called in English C.A.A.C. but due to be reorganised) flies to most major cities. Again it is not easy to book ahead. If you have onward or return international flights they must be reconfirmed *quèdìng* in person at the C.A.A.C. office.

> *Dào (Guǎngzhōu) de xià cì hángbān shì shénme shíhou?*
> When is the next flight to (Canton)?

> *Míngtiān de yǐjīng mǎn le, hòutiàn de yǒu wèizi.*
> Tomorrow's is already full, there are seat on the next day's.

Basic sentences and vocabulary

Where is the (Peace Hotel)?
(Hépíng Fàndiàn) zài nǎr?
Where is there (a post office)?
Nǎr yǒu (yóujú)?
How do I get to (the Friendship Store)?
Dào (Yǒuyì Shāngdiàn) zěnme zǒu?
We've arrived at (the Friendship Store)
(Yǒuyì Shāngdiàn) dào le
Is (the Great Wall) far from here?
(Chángchéng) lí zhèr yuǎn ma?
Do you have ticket(s) to (Canton)?
Yǒu dào (Guǎngzhōu) de piào ma?

go	*qù*
come	*lái*
walk, go to	*zǒu*
from . . . to . . .	*cóng . . . dào . . .*
towards	*wàng*
turn	*guǎi*
here	*zhèr*
there	*nèr/nàr*
where	*nǎr*
intersection, crossroad	*lùkǒu*
traffic lights	*hónglǜdēng*
travel agency	*lǚxíngshè*
guide	*jiǎngjiěyuán*

map	*dìtú*
time-table	*shíkè biǎo*
ticket	*piào*
booking office	*shòupiào chù*
left luggage office	*xínglǐ jìcún chù*
train	*huǒchē*
station	*huǒchē zhàn*
soft sleeper (1st class)	*ruǎnwò*
hard sleeper (2nd class)	*yìngwò*
hard seat (3rd class)	*yìngzuò*
express	*kuàichē*
dining car	*cānchē*
seat	*zuòwèi/wèizi*
bus	*gōnggòng qìchē/qìchē*
bus stop/station	*qìchē zhàn*
trolley bus	*wúguǐ diànchē*
minibus	*miànbāochē*
route no . . .	*. . . lù*
car	*qìchē*
taxi	*chūzūchē*
bicycle	*zìxíngchē*
parking place	*tíngchē chǎng*
plane	*fēijī*
airport	*(fēi) jī chǎng*

6

Shopping

A part from shopping in the big hotels, you will probably have the chance to go to a Friendship Store (*Yǒuyì Shāngdiàn*) and/or a department store (*bǎihuò dàlóu*), both of which are likely to be well-stocked but with goods limited as to quality and variety. In the former, which were originally for foreigners only, you can buy high-quality Chinese silks, cloisonné, jewellery, paintings and furniture as well as imported consumer products. In the latter you will find the kind of things Chinese people buy for daily use — crockery, bedding etc. There are also many smaller specialist shops (for books, for example) and, in recent years, the free markets (*zìyóu shìcháng*). You can bargain over prices in the free markets, but not elsewhere.

Do not be dismayed if your request for a particular item is greeted with a *méi yǒu*, 'there aren't any.' Shop assistants are not noted for their helpfulness to Chinese or to foreigners. Persevere and try out your Chinese — even a little helps a lot in these situations.

The shops are open seven days a week, usually until 6.00 or 7.00 in the evenings, so you will have plenty of opportunities to try out your Chinese.

Hotels, shops and Friendship Stores will normally accept major credit cards including Visa, Mastercharge and American Express, and it is usually possible to change money there as well. The official exchange rate is the same everywhere and there is no point in shopping around to try and get a better deal.

If you find yourself with Renminbi you can use it freely in normal shops and markets, and even Friendship Stores, if pressed, will accept it for Chinese-made goods, apart from jewellery, precious metals, antiques and so on.

Signs you will see:

商店
shāngdiàn
shop

百货大楼
bǎihuò dàlóu
department store

收款台
shōukuǎntái
cashier

元
yuán
¥RMB

角
jiǎo
RMB dime

分
fēn
RMB cent

The payment system in most shops is usually the nineteenth-century cashier booth system. The sales assistant makes out a bill which you take to the cashier's booth (*shōukuǎntái*) for payment. The cashier stamps it and you take it back to the sales assistant, who will exchange it for the goods, which with luck will by then have been wrapped.

The written prices are usually marked as *yuán*, 'dollar', *jiǎo*, 'dime' and *fēn*, 'cent', but spoken as *kuài*, 'dollar', *máo*, 'dime' and *fēn*. Chinese use all three units, so ¥26.75 is *èrshí liù kuài* (or *yuán*) *qī máo* (or *jiāo*) *wǔ* and NOT *èrshí liù kuài qīshí wǔ fēn*. (The last unit is frequently not spoken, e.g. *shíbā kuài wǔ* is ¥18.50. If you want to say ¥18.05 it is expressed as *shíba kuài líng wǔ (fēn)* (=zero dimes+five cents).

Clothes are usually sized by S, M, L, XL, but the actual sizes vary considerably. If you are buying for someone else take along their measurements and a tape measure.

Basic sentences and vocabulary

I'm going shopping	*Wǒ qù mǎi dōngxi*
How much is it?	*Duōshao qián?*
It's too expensive	*Tài guì le*
Can you lower the price a bit?	*Néng piányì diǎn(r) ma?*
I'd like to buy some (perfume)	*Wǒ yào mǎi (xiāngshuǐ)*
I like this one	*Wǒ xǐhuan zhèi ge*
I don't want that one	*Wǒ bú yào nèi ge*
Please give me a receipt	*Qǐng gěi wǒ fā piào*
Have you got a (big/ small/red one)?	*Ní yǒu (dà de/xiǎo de/ hóng de) ma?*

Expensive (one)	*guì (de)*
Cheap (one)	*piányì (de)*
What size?	*Duō dà?*
Too (small)	*tài (xiǎo)*
Even (smaller)	*gèng (xiǎo)*
Can I try it on?	*Kěyǐ shì yí shì ma?*
My (camera) is broken	*Wǒ de (zhàoxiàngjī) huài le*
Can you repair it?	*Néng xiū ma?*
¥RMB (written)	*yuán*
(spoken)	*kuài*
RMB dime (written)	*jiǎo*
(spoken)	*máo*
cent	*fēn*
credit card	*xìnyòng kǎ*
clothes	*yīfu*
silk fabric	*sīchóu*
porcelain	*cíqì*
jade (carvings)	*yùdiāo*
jewellery	*shǒushì*
film (for cameras)	*jiāojuǎn*
battery	*diànchí*
dictionary	*zìdiǎn*
English-language newspapers	*Yīngwén bào*
sweets, candy	*táng* (or *tángguǒ*)
soap	*féizào*
toothbrush	*yáshuā*
toothpaste	*yágāo*
tampons	*wèishēng shuān*
razor	*tìdāo*
razor-blades	*dāopiàn*
Band-Aids	*zhǐxuè jiāobù*

7

Eating

Chinese cuisine has been called the greatest in the world, and whatever one's views on this, it is indisputable that the Chinese are more interested in food than most other cultures are. An enormous amount of time and energy is spent not only on producing, preparing and consuming it, but also on talking about it.

There are numerous restaurants in all the large cities of China, and if you are adventurous enough to leave your hotel and tackle the cuisine of one of these, you could find it an interesting and rewarding experience.

On arrival, you may be asked *Jǐ wèi?*, 'How many (of you)?' (*wèi* is the honorific measure-word used of others). You should answer with the appropriate numeral followed by the non-honorific measure-word *ge* — for example, *sān ge*, 'Three (of us)'.

In some restaurants the staff may attempt to usher you into a special (and more expensive) section reserved for foreigners, and if you want to resist this you can say *Kěyǐ zuò zài zhèr ma?*, 'Can we sit here?', though it might mean having to wait.

To summon the waiter, say *Fúwùyuán*, or *Xiǎojie* (to a waitress). He or she will probably ask *Nǐ yào chī shénme?* 'What do you want to eat?'. Since reading a Chinese menu is out of the question, you can ask for some well-known dishes, or point at dishes you see other people eating and say *Wǒ yào chī nèi ge*, 'I want to eat that.' You could also ask for types of food, for example *Nǐ yǒu yú/jī/zhūròu ma?*. 'Have you got any fish/chicken/pork?' (When Chinese people refer to meat, they usually mean pork, which is the most commonly eaten meat, although beef and — in Northern areas — lamb are also eaten.)

If you are a vegetarian (which can be problematic in China) try saying *Wǒ zhǐ chī sùcài*, 'I only eat vegetarian food.'

By tradition, people in the North tend to eat more *miàn* (wheat-based dishes like noodles, pancakes and steamed bread), whereas in the rest of China the preferred staple is *mǐfàn* (rice).

Chinese typically drink tea *chá* without milk or sugar and in various varieties: jasmine tea *huāchá*, in the north, green tea *lǜchá* and western-style *hóngchá*. Fizzy soft drinks *qìshuǐ* are popular and coffee *kāfēi* is increasingly common.

Alcoholic drinks *jiǔ* include excellent lager-type *píjiǔ*, grape wines *pútaojiǔ*, which tend to be very sweet, and stronger alcoholic drinks such as *Máotái* and other *báijiǔ* (literally, 'white-wine' — but made of various grains and often 60-70% alcohol and very fiery).

The waiter or waitress might ask *Nǐmen yào hē shénme?*, 'What would you like to drink?' and you can reply *Wǒmen yào (sì) píng píjiǔ*, 'We'd like (four) bottles of beer.'

In hotel rooms you will find vacuum flasks of boiled water (*kāi shuǐ*) which it is safe to drink. Although the water in major cities is reckoned to be fit to drink, it is wiser to use only boiled or mineral water.

Cheaper Chinese eating-places are not renowned for their hygiene, so be prepared to take along your own chop-sticks, spoon and cup. The food itself, however, since it is cooked quickly and at high temperatures and eaten at once, should present few health hazards.

A good deal of entertaining is done in hotels and restaurants and most business people will expect to attend at least one banquet during their stay. These can consist of a large number of courses and it would be wise to pace yourself very carefully. The first dish is generally a plate of cold meats *lěngpán* followed by a series of hot dishes and often, at the end, oranges or other fruit. In the North, soup *tāng* may be served as the last course. Rice *mǐfàn* is very much a filler only and may not be served until the meal is well under way.

For most dishes it is normal to help yourself from the middle of the table. To be polite, your Chinese hosts will often help you to food, but if they see you are comfortable with chopsticks *kuàizi*, they may say *Qǐng nǐ súibiàn chī*, 'Please help yourself.'

You may be asked *Yào yòng dāochā ma?*
'Would you like to use a knife and fork'
and can respond *Bú yào, wǒ huì yòng kuàizi*
'No, I can use chopsticks' or *Hǎo, xièxie, bú
huì yòng kuàizi*, 'Yes, thank you, I don't know
how to use chopsticks.'

Signs you will see:

西餐   中餐   餐厅

xīcān   zhōngcān   cāntīng
western restaurant Chinese restaurant restaurant
  (in hotel)

See Appendix for a list of food and drinks

Few foreigners have the chance to eat in a
Chinese home, but if you are invited to a
friend's house it might well be to join in a *jiǎozi*-
making party. *Jiǎozi* are very popular *biànfàn*
'ordinary food' in North China. They are small
pancakes stuffed with meat, vegetables and
seasonings, wrapped into crescent shapes and
then either boiled or steamed. The labour-
intensive process of making them is a social
event almost as important as eating them. You
may be asked *Jīntiān wǎnshang nǐ yǒu kòng(r)
ma?* 'Are you free this evening?'. *Yǒu*, 'Yes'.
Nà, lái wǒ jiā bāo jiǎozi. hǎo bu hǎo? 'Well,
come to my house and make some *jiǎozi* —
OK?' *Hǎo, xièxie*, 'OK. Thanks.'

Chinese meals, *zǎofàn* 'breakfast', *wǔfàn*
'lunch' and *wǎnfàn* 'dinner,' tend to be
earlier than in the West. Lunch and dinner
consist of rice or noodles plus meat and
vegetable dishes, although large hotels have
both western food *Xīcān*, and Chinese
Zhōngcān.

Chinese breakfast is rather more unfamiliar to the westerner. It tends to consist of a bowl of hot rice porridge *zhōu* or *xīfàn*, flavoured with pickled vegetables *pàocài* or shredded dried meat *ròusōng*, plus some buns — *mántou* 'steamed bread roll,' *shāobǐng*, 'sesame seed bun', or other types of bread or pastry. If they are in a hurry, Chinese will grab a *yóutiáo* 'deep-fried dough strip' and some soyabean milk *dòujiāng* from a roadside vendor.

There is a wide variety of regional specialities in China — Mongolian hot-pot *shuànyángròu* in the North, for instance, and also Peking duck *Běijīng kǎoyā*; sweet dumplings in Shanghai; hot spicy, *là*, dishes from Sichuan and of course the snacks known to westerners as 'dim sum' *diǎn xīn* from Canton.

When you wish to leave the restaurant, you can say *Qǐng jié zhàng*, 'Please make out the bill.' Tips *xiǎofèi* are officially not accepted in the PRC but are becoming more common and are normal in Hong Kong and Taiwan.

Basic sentences and vocabulary

What dishes would you like?
> *Nǐmen yào chī shénme cài?*

We'd like . . .   *Wǒmen yào . . .*

What would you like to drink?
> *Nǐmen yào hē shénme?*

Three bottles of beer, two bottles of soft drink and a bottle of *Maotai*
Sān píng píjiǔ, liǎng píng qìshuǐ, yì píng Máotái

Do you have (Peking duck) here?
> *Zhèr yǒu (Běijīng kǎoyā) ma?*

Do you have a menu in English?
> *Yǒu Yīngwén càidān ma?*

Do you like eating Chinese food?
    Nǐ xǐhuān chī Zhōngguó cài ma?
(I like it) very much   *Hěn xǐhūan*
Really delicious   *Zhēn hǎochī*
I'm full   *Wǒ chībǎo le*
Good health   *Zhù nǐ jiànkāng*
Cheers   *Gānbēi*
(literally 'Drink your glass dry')

8

Medical Treatment

Many large hotels, universities, factories and other organisations have their own clinic *yīwùsuǒ*, although there is no guarantee that the doctor will speak English. Ask *Zhèr yǒu yīwùsuǒ ma? Wǒ yào kàn bìng* 'Is there a clinic here? I want to see a doctor.' If there is, the answer will be *Yǒu* and you will be directed there. If the answer is negative, *Méi yǒu*, you will have to ask *Nǎr yǒu yīyuàn?* Where is there a hospital? If you are in contact with your embassy it is sensible to ring the embassy nurse and ask her to recommend a suitable hospital.

On arrival at hospital the first thing is to register, *guàhào*, at the Registration Office, *Guàhào chù*. There you will be asked personal details (see Talking About Yourself), what sort of medical treatment you want (western medicine *xīyào* or Chinese medicine *hōngyào*, medical *nèikē*, surgical *wàikē*, E.N.T. *ěrbíhóukē* etc.) and be asked to pay a fee. Then you will be sent to a consulting room *zhěnshì* to be examined.

After the usual general questions about your background the doctor will ask something like *Nǐ nǎr bú shūfu?* meaning literally 'Where are you unwell?' This is your cue to use one of the phrases below, as appropriate, prefaced by *Wǒ . . .* 'I . . .'. For example you might say *Wǒ fā shāo, lā dùzi* 'I have a fever and diarrhoea.'

If the doctor prescribes medicine *yào* he will give you a prescription *yàofāng* which you take to the pharmacy *yàofáng* (at such times correct tones matter!) The pharmacist will explain the dosage *Yàopiàn měi tiān chī (sān) cì měi cì (liǎng) piàn.* 'Take the tablets (three) times a day, (two) tablets each time.'

Signs you will see:

医院
yīyuàn
hospital

挂号处
guàhàochù
registration office

药房
yàofáng
pharmacy

Chinese doctors tend to be very keen on injections, both for blood tests *yàn xuè* and delivering medication. Many places still use re-usable needles, which, because of inadequate sterilisation and the prevalence of hepatitis, can pose dangers. If you think you may need injections take disposable needles with you. Taking X-rays *àikèsī guāng* is also popular but in some cases you may be exposed to unnecessarily large doses by western standards. If you feel your ailment doesn't warrant an X-ray and if it is suggested, say *Bú bì, bú bì, wǒ hěn kuài jiù huí guó, nǐ zhǐ gěi wǒ diǎnr yào ba*, 'It's not necessary, I'm going back home soon, just give me a little medicine.'

If you need dental attention say *Wǒ yào kàn yá* 'I want to see a dentist' and you will be directed to a hospital dental department *yákē*. If you have toothache point to the appropriate place and say *Zhèr téng* 'It aches here.' The dentist may suggest a filling *Yào bǔ yá* 'You need a filling' but don't confuse this with *bá yá* 'extraction.'

Basic sentences and vocabulary

What's wrong with you?   *Nǐ nǎr bú shūfu?*
My (head) aches   *Wǒ (tóu) téng*
I have a cold   *Wǒ gǎnmào le*
I have a fever   *Wǒ fā shāo le*
I have diarrhoea   *Wǒ lā dùzi*
I have (heart trouble)   *Wǒ yǒu (xīnzàngbìng)*
I need to see a doctor   *Wǒ yào kàn bìng*
Where is the hospital/clinic?
                Yīyuàn/yīwùsuǒ zài nǎr?
When does the clinic open?
            Yīwùsuǒ shénme shíhou kāi mén?
Does it hurt here?   *Zhèr téng ma?*
How long have you had it?
                Yǒu duō cháng shíjiān le?
It started (yesterday)   *Cóng (zuótiān) kāishǐ de*
Are you allergic to (penicillin)?
            Nǐ duì (qīngméisù) guòmǐn ma?

No	*bù*
clinic	*yīwùsuǒ*
hospital	*yīyuàn*
doctor	*yīshēng/dàifu*
nurse	*hùshi*
dentist	*yáyī*
Chinese (traditional) medicine	*zhōngyī*
Western medicine	*xīyī*
head	*tóu*
eye	*yǎnjīng*
ear	*ěrduo*

throat	*hóulóng*
stomach	*wèi*
heart	*xīnzàng*
liver	*gān*
blood	*xuè, xiě*
X-ray	*àikèsī guāng*
blood test	*yàn xuè*
urine test	*yàn niào*
injection	*dǎ zhēn, zhùshè*
medicine	*yào*
tablets	*yàopiàn*
prescription	*yàofāng*
thermometer	*tǐwēnjì*
be allergic to . . .	*duì . . . guòmǐn*
aspirin	*āsīpǐlín*
penicillin	*qīngméisù*
a cold, flu	*gǎnmào*
diarrhoea	*lā dùzi*
constipated	*(yǒu diǎnr) biànmì*
fever	*fā shāo*
tooth	*yá*
filling	*bǔ yá*
extraction	*bá yá*

Appendices

NUMERAL SYSTEM

The system is very straightforward compared to many languages. 0-10 are as follows:

0	*líng*
1	*yī* (pronounced *yāo* as part of serial no., phone no. etc.)
2	*èr*
	liǎng (used with measure + noun)
3	*sān*
4	*sì*
5	*wǔ*
6	*liù*
7	*qī*
8	*bā*
9	*jiǔ*
10	*shí*

The only tricky point is to remember that 2 items is *liǎng* + measure + noun, e.g. two people is *liǎng ge rén*, two books is *liǎng běn shū* and so on, but in larger numbers 2 is *èr*, so 22 people is *èrshí èr ge rén*. Where there is no measure 2 is normally *èr*.

Numbers from 11-99 are formed by combinations of the above:

11	*shíyī*
12	*shíèr*
19	*shíjiǔ*
20	*èrshí*
21	*èrshí yī*
30	*sānshí*
99	*jiǔshí jiǔ*

Higher numbers use *bǎi* hundred, *qiān* thousand, *wàn* ten thousand and *yì* hundred million. There is no single word for million, which is expressed as *bǎiwàn* (100 x 10,000) and this makes large numbers more difficult to grasp immediately.

100	*yìbǎi*
103	*yìbǎi líng sān*
148	*yìbǎi sìshí bā*
200	*èrbǎi/liǎngbǎi*
1,000	*yìqiān*
2,000	*liǎngqiān/èrqiān*
10,000	*yíwàn*
6,583,492	*liùbǎi wǔshí bā wàn* *sānqiān sìbǎi jiǔshí èr*

Fractions are expressed as . . . *fēn zhī* . . .

¾   *sì fēn zhī sān*

and percentages similarly with *bǎi fēn zhī* . . .

32%   *bǎi fēn zhī sānshí 'èr*

Ordinal numbers (first, second etc.) are formed by inserting *dì* before the cardinal number. *Dì yī* is 'first' *dì'èr* is 'second' and so on. In commonly used words the *dì* may be omitted, so 'third floor' is *sān lóu*.

DATES AND TIMES

Dates are expressed with *nián* year, *yuè* month and *rì* or *hào* day, in that order. The year is always followed by *nián*.

23rd September 1986:
> *yī jiǔ bā liù nián jiǔ yuè èrshí sān rì*

Questions normally use *jǐ* but the vaguer *shénme shíhou* 'when' can also be used:
Which year? (lit. nineteen eighty what?)
> *yī jiǔ bā jǐ nián?*

Which month? *jǐ yuè*
What date? *jǐ hào*

The months are:

January	*yī yuè*
February	*èr yuè*
March	*sān yuè*
April	*sì yuè*
May	*wǔ yuè*
June	*liù yuè*
July	*qī yuè*
August	*bā yuè*
September	*jiǔ yuè*
October	*shí yuè*
November	*shíyī yuè*
December	*shí'èr yuè*

Duration of time in months is expressed by adding the measure *ge* so *sān yuè* is March but *sān ge yuè* is three months.

Days of the week use *lǐbài* or *xīngqī* plus a numeral or *tiān/rì* (for Sunday).

Sunday	*xīngqī tiān*
Monday	*xīngqī yī*
Tuesday	*xīngqī èr*
Wednesday	*xīngqī sān*
Thursday	*xīngqī sì*
Friday	*xīngqī wǔ*
Saturday	*xīngqī liù*

Again *jĭ* is used for the question form:
  Which day (of the week)? *xīngqī jĭ?*
and the duration form takes the measure *ge*
  three weeks *sān ge xīngqī*

Hours and minutes as clock times are expressed by *diăn* and *fēn* with *bàn* and *kè* used for the half hour and the quarters. Generally nothing is used to indicate 'past' as in 'twenty past five,' just the hours and minutes is sufficient. Minutes 'to' the hour is expressed by *chà* 'lack' in either of the positions shown below. However, this tends only to be used for times from about ten to the hour: up to a quarter to is treated as past the previous hour. Where it is a straight hour with no minutes *zhōng* 'clock' is often added.

11 o'clock	*shíyī diăn (zhōng)*
three minutes past 11	*shíyī diăn sān fēn*
ten past 11	*shíyī diăn shí fēn*
quarter past 11	*shíyī diăn yí kè/shíwŭ fēn*
twenty five past 11	*shíyī diăn èrshí wŭ fēn*
half past 11	*shíyī diăn bàn*
twenty to 12	*shíyī diăn sìshí fēn*
quarter to 12	*shíyī diăn sān kè/sìshí wŭ fēn*
ten to twelve	*chà shí fēn shí'èr diăn* (*shí'èr diăn chà shí fēn*)
two minutes to 12	*chà liăng fēn shí'èr diăn* (*shí'èr diăn chà liăng fēn*)

Since *diăn* (literally 'dot') is a measure, two o'clock is *liăng diăn*; never use *èr*.

For official times, like airline times, Chinese use the 24 hour clock, but in ordinary speech they use the 12 hour clock, like us, plus one of the following, where it is necessary to indicate a.m. or p.m.

early morning	*zǎoshang*
morning (8-12 o'clock)	*shàngwǔ*
noon	*zhōngwǔ*
afternoon	*xiàwǔ*
evening	*wǎnshàng*
night	*yèli*
6.30 a.m.	*zǎoshang liù diǎn bàn*
5.45 p.m.	*xiàwǔ wǔ diǎn sān kè*

For duration minutes *fēn* and quarters *kè* are used in the same way as clock time but *zhōng* is added

| five minutes | *wǔ fēn zhōng* |
| three quarters of an hour | *sān kè zhōng* |

Hours are expressed by the number + measure *ge* + *zhōngtou* or *xiǎoshí* and half *bàn* is treated like a number. With *xiǎoshí*, the measure *ge* is optional.

| two hours | *liǎng ge zhōngtou* |
| half an hour | *bàn ge xiǎoshí* |

but note

| one and a half hours | *yí ge bàn xiǎoshí* |

COUNTRIES AND CURRENCIES

The People's Republic of China	*Zhōnghuá Rénmín Gònghéguó*
China	*Zhōngguó*
RMB	*Rénmínbì*
Australia	*Àodàlìyà*
Australian $	*Àoyuán*
Canada	*Jiānádà*
Canadian $	*Jiāyuán*
France	*Fǎguó*
French franc	*Fǎláng*
Germany	*Déguó*
German mark	*Mǎkè*
Hong Kong	*Xiānggǎng*
Hong Kong $	*Gǎngbì*
Italy	*Yìdàlì*
Lira	*Lǐlā*

Japan	Rìběn
Japanese Yen	Rìyuán
New Zealand	Xīnxīlán
New Zealand $	Xīnxīlán yuán
Spain	Xībānyá
Peseta	Bǐsàitǎ
United Kingdom	Yīngguó
£ Sterling	Yīngbàng
United States	Měigúo
U.S.$	Měiyuán

WEIGHTS AND MEASURES

China now officially uses the metric system but traditional weights and measures are still used. There is scope for confusion between the two, so, if it is important, make sure which system is being used.

Traditional		*Metric*	
lǐ	0.3 mile, 0.5 km.	gōnglǐ	kilometre
chǐ	13.1 in. 0.33 m	mǐ, gōngchǐ	metre
cùn	1.3 inch, 3.3 cm.	gōngfēn	centimetre
jīn	1.1 lb., 500g	gōngjīn	kilogram
liǎng	1.8 oz., 50g	kè	gram

FOOD & DRINK

Traditionally, Chinese do not drink milk nor eat dairy products, although these are becoming available. They do eat almost anything else that is conceivably edible (and a certain amount that is not — if in doubt do not ask!).

Basic foods

boiled rice	mǐfàn
noodles	miàn (tiáo)
bread	miànbāo
steamed bread	mántou

meat	*ròu*
pork	*(zhū) ròu*
beef	*niúròu*
lamb	*yángròu*
chicken	*jī*
duck	*yā*
fish	*yú*
shrimp, prawn	*xiā*
egg	*jīdàn*
soup	*tāng*
bean curd	*dòufŭ*
rice porridge	*zhōu, xīfàn*
vegetables	*shūcài*
Chinese cabbage	*báicài*
tomato	*xīhóngshì*
cucumber	*huángguā*
potato	*tŭdòu/mălíngshŭ*
bamboo shoot	*zhúsŭn*
aubergine	*qiézi*
mushroom	*mógu*
garlic	*suàn*

Flavours & flavourings

salty	*xián*
sweet	*tián*
bitter	*kŭ*
sour	*suān*
hot spicy	*là*
salt	*yán*
soy sauce	*jiàngyóu*
chilli powder	*làjiāo fěn*
monosodium glutamate	*wèijīng*

Dishes & cooking methods

dish (cooked food)	*cài*
hors d'oeuvres	*lěng pán*
hot sour soup	*suān là tāng*
noodle soup	*tāng miàn*
Peking duck	*Běijīng kăoyā*

Mongolian hot-pot	*shuàn yángròu*
crispy fried chicken & peanuts	*gōngbǎo jīdīng*
braised (fish) in brown sauce	*hóngshāo (yú)*
sweet and sour (pork)	*gúlāo (ròu)*
(chicken) casserole	*shāguō (jī)*
sweet and sour (fish)	*tángcù (yú)*
hot spicy bean curd	*mápó dòufǔ*
(pork shreds) in hot garlic sauce	*yúxiāng (ròusī)*
mushu pork (pork with egg)	*mùxu ròu*
saute beef with onions	*cōngtóu chǎo niúròu*
fried noodles	*chǎo miàn*
spring rolls	*chūn juǎnr*
dumplings	*jiǎozi*
steamed stuffed bun	*bāozi*

Drinks

tea	*chá*
green tea	*lǜ chá*
jasmine tea	*huā chá*
Indian style tea	*hóng chá*
coffee	*kāfēi*
water	*shuǐ*
mineral water	*kuàngquán shuǐ*
carbonated soft drink	*qìshuǐ*
Coca cola	*kěkǒu kělè*
orange juice	*júzhī*
milk	*niúnǎi*
alcoholic drink	*jiǔ*
beer	*píjiǔ*
wine	*pútaojiǔ*
white spirit	*báijiǔ*
Shaoxing rice wine	*Shàoxīng jiǔ*
Maotai (strong white spirit)	*Máotái jiǔ*

MEASURE WORDS

See p.19 for explanation of when measure words need to be used. Below are some common measures and the sort of nouns they are used with.

ge	people; the general measure used where there is no specific one
běn	books and bound publications
bì	amounts of money
céng	storey of building, layer
chǎng	sporting events, performances of plays, films etc
cì	recurring events — wars, meetings; very common as verbal measure meaning times — *sān cì* 'three times'
fēng	letters
jiā	enterprises — shops, hotels, companies
jià	aeroplanes, machines, items with frame-work
jiān	room
jiàn	items of clothing, luggage, incidents
kuài	piece of — land, cake etc.; dollar — basic unit of money
lóu	floor, storey of building
shuāng	pair of, e.g. shoes
suǒ	houses and other buildings
tiáo	long thin items: rivers, roads, stockings
wèi	formal measure for people (see *ge* above)
zhāng	flat items: tables, maps, newspapers, stamps
zhī	pencils, pens